Dominion: God of This World

Rev – D
First Edition

Joseph Leo Hickey III

Cover illustrations by Joseph Leo Hickey III.

Melodium
House

www.MelodiumHouse.com
joseph@melodiumhouse.com

Introductory Information

Harmonie and Liefie are wild and free and very much alive!

It is a time of danger, and the voices that should be outraged shudder in silence, but if they are silent by choice, or by threat or by ignorance is known only to God.

After the world quivers under the yoke of its own governments, who seized a perfect opportunity to gain control, the United Nations now holds dominion over the entire world.

The young couple Harmonie and Liefie who met at an airport at the age of seventeen, now conspire to fly to Costa Rica, one of the few nations that has not completely shut its borders to get married.

They seek to find a home together far away from the worlds they had known in their youth.

Key:

Harmonie, Liefie,
Liefie + Harmonie, *Sanger,* <u>All</u>

Si te vas yo también me voy
Si me das yo también te doy
Mi amor
Bailamos hasta las diez
Hasta que duelan los pies
-Enrique Iglesias, Duele el Corazon

I took my Power in my Hand —
And went against the World —
-Emily Dickinson

But if anyone does not provide for his own, and especially for those of his household, he has denied the faith and is worse than an unbeliever.
-1 Timothy 5:8

CD #11

my dreams swallowed me whole

waiting in the news, anticipating,
anger and bitter news
Matthias perched outside the window,
without fear,
knowing that his spirit is enraged and
impassioned,
waiting for us to learn what will happen to
our futures ,
the tears within my heart already begin to
swell and to burst,
not knowing what disaster might befall us,
one pain follows another,
each day follows the night
and the world edges closer to the place
where it will never find rest in its prison,
i have dreams of my own, about dancing and dreaming

here in this place, Rafa is ready to guide his armies in war,
Angels unleashed in their wrath and defence of those who
exist under their union and their light,

I am a guarded soul, a being elevated as if to the heights
of the stars, reaching out as a pilgrim soul,
The book of my life is open for all to read and understand,
what is the point of hiding anything?
My voice is unlimited, unchained, like the melody,
I have a heart wounded by the arrows of my bitter enemies,
the times exhausted,
but here my husband and I wait in the USCIS office,
waiting for news, a decision, anything, for even the time on the clock to
expire and guide me somewhere, if in that very world I can breathe,
we had spent that summer traveling together,
we found each other, but we never found a permanent home,
we only found each other in separate nations,
the seas calling us to be together forever,
But the one who had Dominion over this world,

always deigned to keep us so far apart,
unable to lift our hearts to touch each other,
but the world we knew, would always reject us,

we were called into the office and knew the wait was finally over
news about our future, where we were going to be,
if we could be together in the same nation would all be decided now,
I held my hopes close to me like the life growing inside my womb,
All the future held together by a thread, so fragile,
I had never wanted to leave South Africa, until the day I learned I was
pregnant,
now all I can think about is the
tangled crowds, weaving through their destruction,
the one who broke into my home and tried to rape me,
South Africa is not a nation, in that hollow place there is no order at all,
All the world belongs to Christ, and his sceptre rules it with ultimate power,
hammering down with an iron fist until mercy finally breaks through,
breaking down the walls forever, which have always kept us so far apart,

the USCIS officer walked into the office with a grim look on his
face,

"i'm sorry, i'm denying Harmonie's green card" he said as the tears began
to swell in my eyes.

he said that "my extremist views against the President of the
United States,
and his decree to slay all the birds" and my "opposition to this decree"
made the President intervene directly and that they've been ordered not to
approve
my request for permanent residency and
that i had 60 days to leave the country,

walking into the sunlight which no longer warmed my face,
when panic sets in, the world spins faster
and out of control and into a place of never finding rest again,
I have a heart inside that grows in vengeance, with sweet hymns,
sung for the dead all across the world itself,
and then I finally realized when the dawn rose above the world,
that the truth in our very veins was growing each day,
no matter how tightly we were squeezed,

our castles of stone surrounded us,
protecting us from the coming of all the shadows,
knowing that my breath surrounds all the oceans,
and the Lord of this world, would only try to tighten his grip
on even my song,,
but then suddenly, Matthias, appeared and i was thrilled with excitement
despite the darkness in this very world
and he told me of the calm and gentle songs,
that were sung far away in the winds of Costa Rica,
a place i would never visit until i die,
i know that before i die, my Liefie and i will pack up our things
and go to airport to meet in Costa Rica,
but really the second we leave our homes,
we are actually dead,
we had passed away, slain by worlds that never understood us,
the Dominion over even our authority to breathe,
was stolen from us,
the Dominion over our homes
was expropriated without compensation,
our currency was destroyed without asking us,
we were blamed for the crimes of our ancestors
and then the boiling world blew over with anger
toward us, not understanding
our hardware or even our programmed path
or software,
the nightmares of the past haunted us
forever in dreams that swallowed us with
empathy, shielding us from the nightmares,
but now in this very moment,
after my Green Card was denied,
i knew that nothing would shield me from the
nightmare, the darkness of a world enshrined in pain,
the love of a mother for her unborn child,
is unmatched, and the failure to provide for her
young family and to protect her son like a shield
from the wicked men in masks,
is overwhelming in its fear,
in trepidation for even moving forward,
will. prevent me from accomplishing anything
at all, including the glorious breath,
i always laboured so hard to earn in this world

after so many years i finally earned my right
to breathe, but now it was forced away
from me by criminals in masks,
by vicious demons who haunt our world
and claw through the sides and seams
of our castles like horror villains,
unstoppable, nothing will contain them
the villains of our story,
will never stop until we are dead
hold me in your arms like the anthem of the future
because at least this moment is for us,
my veins are bursting with passion,
even now

335

the streets of Durban, overflowing
with the waves of the ocean which
not one single soul ever notices,
i allow myself to be swallowed by those very waves,
which entice all the worlds,

the dead-end life of this world,
we surrender our hopes,
and resign ourselves with faith,
that one day there will be a way out,
unemployment rate nigh fifty percent,
the lives we lived had banished the stars
which we should all be gazing at,
the world is rife with opportunities
to change, and we are always deemed so lucky,
if we even have a job, or otherwise stay here,
without a home,
or otherwise amass great amounts of debt which
we will never be able to pay back,
my anthem sings throughout the world,
it always has,
the winds of my aching heart,
like a song, like a stone that rolls through a stream,
at the complete mercy
of the oceans, which all the worlds connect to,

in their darkness, there is a calling of shadows,
temptation to fall into these shadows,
but we would never escape,
yet here i am,
these waves overwhelming me, soaked in their embrace
despair that overcomes a soul, when it can no longer move
on its own accord,
i once had hope for a future which I held and cherished,
i held it as a many coloured light which in my hands,
the stone of light, had the power to light up all the world,
glowing and illuminating every dark room where I stood,
but this light of the stars was seized and now I will never
find it again,
this very light is now lost forever, was stolen by the villain
who broke into my home one night and threatened to kill me,
the hope of the future was always so fragile,
a life filled with fear and trauma that overflows this world,
where because we are all in the same precarious position,
there is no one here who will listen,
the desperate but vicious winds of this world,
against my patient but eternal watchfulness,
all i will ever do now is wait for the world
to flee from my vision,
so that I could no longer see this world,
dressed in my pain, wearing those very stars on my skin,
memories of dear family members who had all died
or fled the nation, and here I am walking these streets
alone, forcibly abandoned by every soul I had ever held dear,
including my Liefie, who I hadn't heard from since my phone was
stolen, if these oceans collapse under my heart,
there will be no way to stop sinking, there is no limit too deep to sink

the crowds through the streets, clattering voices,
melding together as one, blending
indistinguishable from all others,
the Liturgy of the Birds and Stars,
flowing on forward with peace
in their understanding of the very breath of heaven,
the memories of times long past
have inebriated my scars, washed them in euphoria,

11

so that I understand that even covered in scars,
there is a place to find healing
and one day the scars will remind us that healing is possible,
but political forces are forever marching through these avenues,
and I remember the days of my youth,
constant reminders of my education,
the future calling me, buried in books
reading about the past while dreaming about the future,
realizing how hopeless it all was and how powerless I am always
to save this nation,
to resist pain,

the weariness within this world
from resisting sleep,
always tempted to never wake up again, nights spent alone, gazing up
toward ten thousand stars,
hearts always pressed forward toward the future,
the sinister forces
at work in the world
will surround our island of light,
capsize all ships that try to
reach our island,
so that not a single soul
seeking refuge here will
ever hope to survive,
my bitter bones erupt
with passion and ingest
all the fear of what
is outside their control
the mighty waves that surround our paradise,
caving in every moment until we can no longer hope
we are surrounded on all sides by the ministers
of violence,

336

dreams pass me by
like strangers
in the night,

the life of eternal
mornings grow in silence
the Wise Man

the Wise Man warned us,
about the unprecedented
winds of the deplorable
ache in all bones,
that united, call us
and follow us in their panic,

the call of the wild winds approaches
from all sides, greets me
in moments when i fear
the very uncertainty of
the time and its vicious cycle
of control, the doors locked
and walls closed around us,
frequent and painful,
knowledge that we will never
be able to move from one place to
another, our own agency within this world
stripped from us,
bridled and unmoved,
the Shipwrecked that
finds us, on an island
we will never escape,
where all I can do is shout
to the wind
which will carry me far away
into the shadows of panic,
greater is my pain in my heart,
than my own agency
or power in pain,

when forever comes for me,
i stand in the same place,
the same place i have always stood,
never shaking my original purpose,
since my first moment in this earth,
darkness invoked in syllables of

the night,
the ground which was once stable,
will begin to collapse underneath my feet,
feel for me now in your deepest heart,
goals in hearts collapsing as well,
forsaking their original purpose,
forever glowing in the night
toward a future, no longer held in the arms
of calmness or light,

the streets echo with the same song
they have always had,
these worlds, collapse as we fall
and we fall into these other worlds,
the side of my heart wounded,
panic setting in,
and taking over, resigning to this panic,
falling face first into this nightmare,
where all we can do is surrender to its
whisper,
glow in its night,
arms outstretched reaching for the sky,
a surrender and a call,
and reaching motion, for
what might never consume us,
for the dreadful panic in veins
to implode eventually,
the sun rising over this world and each
verse of my sung understood,
each life, unbent,
each soul will be rent into pieces,
into many different hearts,
that are spread throughout this world,
growing with me in purpose,
and holding its song
close like an anthem of the quiet birds,
that fly through all these skies,
(maybe someday they will reach yours)
the future forever bleak, lives always struck by tragedy,
one step at a time, flowing forward in truth,
and memory, in life and in pain,

in desperate anthems of life,
my ticket to nowhere burns,
and i never take the train,
the city of my heart flowing forward in
its memory,
of pain and panic on my skin,
the risks taken, the lives overturned,
the hearts outstretched and torn,
miracles are found at every turn in
this world where we hold forever on our skin,
burning the light of the chasm of eternity,
where we can never cross
one side to the other,
memories of my parents burned,
and i miss every light in this world,
burning in the already stricken
love, from my heart,
and there are many miles left on our journey,
the soles of my feet are worn as we
progress through this journey,
the harsh display of despair,
will meet with us eventually,
all i can do is put it off and hope it
never reaches me,
dream with me on the floor of your
asphalt, tread with me forever,
in the anthem of what was only
believed in dreams,
the grace of the treading heart on
the floor of oceans,
holding all it needs,
never letting go,
no matter how desperately hot
its crevices become,
in the eternal motion of falling,
growing in the moment of
anticipation, for whatever might
become of our precious world,
the TV wild at night, showing us things
we never believed or understood,
dwelling forever in the motion of eternal

love, havens of peace
and glory, following us
wherever we can think and understand that
we are truly the ones who always
believed in what we felt in dreams,

my warrior-soul, drew all its strength,
from a poem, the heat of its hurricane,
imploding on all who cannot stand,
my floating heart, will
someday find a place of rest,
somewhere in this world,
or perhaps, elsewhere, in
some other world
the fragrance of this world
has become bitter to me,
where movement is impossible,
where the freedom to express
my soul grows dimmer each moment,
where in all moments i hold myself
and all eternity inside a single
syllable of this poem,
you speak to me in Spanish,
you tell me secrets of the world
and of all worlds,
together we will dance all night, until
the world has one more heart,
one more soul to hold,
one more life inside,
one more night to survive,
the grave danger we face,
in a world where the angels
fade and the lights all fall from the sky,
guiding us no more as they did before,
but i follow you through this night
and you know i always will,

my love, your truth surrounds all
the world, in its venom,
in its credulity, in its precious
and unbelievable impassioned speech,

this world belongs to us,
now and always has, a home to have,
a home to hold,
a grace to pursue an uncreated light,
to meld, to grasp, and to enshrine
in our lamps, to pasture,
in this night which we persevere through forever, after and always
in the light of the morning
we follow the lamps in the river,
guiding us to the ocean it connects to,
the secret and narrow path,
which we follow takes us to what we hope for, but what we've only seen face
to face in dreams.
i swear, the rest we've only seen in whispers, and we could not process these
thoughts in our minds,
they were too much for us,
too much to believe, too much to hold,
too much to find in this world
where the rest of everything is only cold,
we treasure what we've found,
we never let it go,
the path winds on, through the mountains,
through all kind of treacherous land,
but it takes us where we know
we always wanted to go,
 breathe with me, above a concrete world,
where nothing is solid enough and it all slowly fades

337

the bravest days of our lives
when we confronted our mistakes without delay,
when memory burns love into our minds and life thrives in
inspiring motions of a passionate muse,
waiting here for the end of all time of course,
this life burns forever in my heart,
with uncertainty,
love calls me forever,
my life fading in
and empty void of chaotic dreams,
be my vision

when my eyes cannot clearly see
the spaces in the sky
that are empty
where all the birds used to fly,

be with me in the night,
the morning calls me forever,
the victory forever in my heart

the streets are filled with empty souls, buying and selling,,
treading the floors of theses streets with passion in every step,
always so much that can be taken from me,
my pursuit of love,
my pursuit of nothing
but vibrant but beautiful noises
within this world,
but every step and every decibel rings out with beauty,
never finding any confidence of my ability
to stand my own ground
until my feet are held to these very fires that burn down my world,
the graven images of our past mistakes haunt us,
now and forever, the life of the world to come gives us the hope that springs
forward always into the wings of tomorrow,
the last and desperate greeting wind
of each powerful utterance
of a single word,
of a single poem
of all words and all poems,
of power meant to be held and stirred within us, growing forever in its spin
and swell

one day the words will come to me
and i will be able to
fly through the world,
not with sight and feeling,
but with words,
bold and always bursting out,
unrestrained, untrained and wild,
courageous in the night
as the stars that never fall down to earth,
as the campaign against the birds thickens,

the President of the United States,
was powerless to slay them all,
  their wings, their wind
their very vision was overwhelming
usurping the whole world
and installing new governments of the hearts,
blowing over those who thought they would never be toppled,
with the simplest gush and torrent of their
fired flight,
each moment for me passes slowly and
vividly, unstoppable,
careless and vividly detailed as well
in its memory,
give to me what you have never
believed in,
your hopes that you have forgotten,
for I am the tired masses,
not only of my community but
of this nation and every nation
and of the whole world,
one human nature that all of us share,
being pressed forward in the light of peace
while living under light and vicious
fireworks of almighty bombs,
here we are treading slowly and bravely in this same night, cadence of love,
peace and our now shared destiny,
if the world is to burn in uncontrollable fires,
then assuredly I will follow you,
if my blessed hope, lost with the peace of myself, i lost when my soul died,
hope is the reason and the anchor of
all wayward souls, the reset for all
of the panic and chaos in this world
where destiny drives me forward
in the anchor of all created things,
holding on this love, almighty and vividly divine,
the light of bombs could not help but be quenched inside the soaked
absorbing blanket of hope which completely surrounded it,
saving those in the shadows,
the human life of ours presses forward
through with eternal love
we all are guests,

trampled over by a world that
was never truly our home,
and we craved escape from this shell,
this hollow hell, we call day to day life,
the loneliness which we crawl into
against the gentle flutter of the breeze
in which can hear day by day,
the always present call of the light,
the justice of finding a light where
we never knew we would find it,
lighting up the room,
leading a path to a place
where we can take our rightful place
at the side of those who came before
in the light of all my peaceful
cantor,
today I dream of a better place away,
always, never understanding the power of governments,
when they thrust me away from my home,
when love is no longer acknowledged,
when. the halls of life are no longer braved,
but we stay in these rooms,
echoing words of hate
from a book we are forced to read
about a life we will be forced to live,
and we will always be crushed completely by our missed opportunities within
this world,
the memory of worlds long ago,
where we stood here, captivated by the love of souls alone,
of greater life calling us,
where at the very least we
can sit here and contemplate what might
happen in the future,
the undisputed triumph of words
unleashed throughout the world,
finding a gentle place on your shelf,
hearts guided to a place of solace,
Liefie, if this side of the world,
if this empty parking lot,
if this very asphalt, feels tangible,
as if i could hold this existence in my hands

and squeeze out its juices,
an existence that tangible is all i ever demanded out of my life,
my crawling and cyclical heart,
the dawning of my soul
treading, but through the spaces
where my soul used to be
before it too fled away with those birds,
that the President sought to slay,
viciously and cruelly,
in his chamber of tortures, his house of delusions, crater of a lonely heart,
power grasped once will not easily be let go again,
the dense layers of my heart
and of all hearts
that stand here,
hoping at the very least to find a way away
from these shores,
but are there any ships coming?
was my heart always destined to
do nothing but sit and wait?
a daughter of destiny approaching suddenly,
with all my brothers and sisters,
we do nothing but wait in the quest
sounds of all woods, settling my mind
cleansing it, greeting it with the gentle
words it always wanted to hear,
the lifetime of my life growing deeper
into the menacing and depth of
lungs filled with love
and ready to exhale and flood all worlds

338

the emphatic song in my
heart of passion,
waiting here still,
for the taste of forever,
for the paradise of all passing time
when invoked to betray the world,
capsizing all ships,
in this sea that we observe
from far away,

believing in what is never reachable,
reaching for what is never understood,
follow me into the void,
to the place where the birds have
flown to,
generous and flowing with
danger, retribution of passion,
finding its fulfilment, always
in all motions coming here
where it meets its ultimate fulfilment,
burst through with me
to the other side through these walls
that surround us,
preventing us from meeting the other,
growing forever in the anthem
of love followed by ancient poems,
words that follow us all,
wherever we go, unable to escape,
the life in my heart treads on forward
through all dark trenches,
follow me into the embers of
that fire which transforms all worlds
all i ever wanted was to be with
you, and in this quiet place,
find my heart unstrung,
free and finally at very last untethered,
all i wanted was the power to sit here and write,
to become all joys to all people,
to have the power to express my brave mind, with those who
cannot stand their own ground,
when strength is plowing on forever,
the anthem of our lives,
where in this desperate place,
the birds hold their council,
and discuss what happened to the world,
through chirps and flapping of wings,
the wind from these very wings like the wrath of the world,
overflowing and certain,
present in the arms all who are held,
of my mind rushing through the world,
with the thoughts of these same birds united

to mine,
the gracious winds of time, forever
a howl in the air,
an eternal sound resonating through all
in the spring of eternity,
the governments pressing their iron fists to
the walls of the world,
could no longer reach these birds or stars,
they had all run away to San Jose,
my precious heart running
through this desolate world
in its veracious twist of the same fate,
if you hold me,
know that i am yours forevermore,
and that in the ringing of ears of these
same winds, our goals never achieved,
our hands are never outplayed,
at the last moment
the tides of the ocean, the underdog
now is the victor,
the gracious sighs in my life
were always flowing forward toward desire of growing
passionate
of the fabled nations
always glowing forward in their light
and in their desire to become more
and to forget the mistakes of
the transparent pasts

i see through all of these things,
growing forever in poverty,
with the world, forgetting souls
as the world burns,
my world burns when a soul burns,
grow with me through all of things,
the precious heart we hold,
flows through all worlds in its truth,
my memory struck by a sudden lightning,
forcing me to stay stagnant in this world,
never move or improve,
my vision struck by a sudden blindness,

but only then can I really see,
now blind to my own desires,
i can be here for you,
clawing forward in the nation on
toward whatever flows through me,
flowing through you as well,
if the patience in my heart
can outlast time,
where will it be then?
if all time moves on forward,
who will be the anthem of my joy,
the reality of tensions in hearts
resounding, growing with me forever
into the hope that we always hoped to hold,
my always is who you are,
my greatest love, falling into you,
in the tempest, always glowing,
always perfected by the storms,
the waves of the roaring seas,
words flow through me like water,
like the rescue of all hearts,
the very day that I no longer feel,
is the day I no longer live,
when the world ceases to feel,
there will no longer be a hope in this world
left to give,
the bright morning of all these worlds
coming together in one moment,
the tension of my precious will
in my mind
always an anthem, never ceasing to be
a song, to live is to grasp the sunlight,
clenching it tightly with both hands,
squeezing, never letting it go,
or having any desire at all to do so,
my warrior heart in its present
ocean, one with all things,
here we stand in the world,
breakers of hearts

339

my life is
a long and frightful journey,
a path tread through the stars,
through the light of
the dim starlight
we find our path,
somehow here,
beautiful and dreadful
as the morning light,
the lights that guide us
have their own souls,
their own wills,
their own twists and turns
as they guide us
on our desperate
and pilgrim path,
through this place which we stand
the time has changed so much
and we find ourselves
one with the breeze
and passing time,
in the sense that we cannot
hold on even in our hands
a single moment or convince
it to stay,
the joy of walking through the library,
i was never the master
of my own breath,
my chaotic trembling voice
through this world
would tread through the
endless fields
where the oceans
once again have given up
their tempest
and yielded to a calmer nature,
the world was always calling me
to crawl through its crevice,
the light of my mind,
flowed forward in all times and places,

destined to sing for some greater song, which I would only know
in some dream which
had passed long ago out of all
memory,
only recalled by God,
who in his truth and compassion
had well hidden things from us that
might disturb our hearts,
the distant view of the mountains
peaking forth somewhere,
I stand here as a pure soul,
heaven greets me in its light,
life follows me in its morning
of generous gifts,
offered to us like grace,
pouring out like a stream of
water, cutting through
all of the nightmares,
the winds still call to me,
because somewhere I know
the gust of wind
was caused by the birds flapping
their wings so many miles away,
now reaching us,
because no one can truly escape
these winds,
torrential storms,
rains falling all around us,
and we desire to become whole
out of the broken pieces that we
once were,
my drenched mind
in these same waters
reaches through
and feels everything,
united in precious love
with those who understand us,
because they took
the time to listen
to truly hear the story
of lives broken,

of kingdoms overthrown,
of love torn,
of powers never known,
walls surrounding us,
holding us in place,
the life of the world
is so brilliant that we will never escape,
the life of its glow,
the reign of its soul,
the greater the gift,
the more we become whole
after so many years
of torment and pain,
the whispers we hear
will lead us again,
to a path that we'll find
somewhere in the dark,
leading us home,
and me to your heart

340

when i arrive at my destination,
called by a heart drawing us together
in this story, my fettered mind,
my redemption found in
the powerful desire that seizes me by the heart, grasps me withouts
hesitation,
and my only want is to be called
by the name by the voice in the rain,
the last fallen memory,
it's anthem unhinged,

the kings of the world, in their disarray,
sided with the darkness, power always over-sprung,
the morning sunrise, breaking the veil of monotony,
flaying forward into the future of my love for a world that
has so quickly slipped away, taking up arms to defend what
we've loved,
casting out all the past dreams that we've forgotten and
outgrown,

bending down and laying down crowns and thrones,

341

Frozen Earth,
we tread, hoping
one night to carve a path out
of this bitter cold air
which clings to us,
meanwhile we are frozen,
here where we no longer have true
agency to move
the scars
passing slowly
reaching out
for a promise
but not a guarantee
a life here is stagnant
take me away from the world
that clenches me
holds me tightly,

buries me eternally
my reach is extended but hindered
my life is broken across the oceans leading you aimlessly where you
will
never find me, except in whispers
the absolution within
my glowing heart
and struck by inspiration
finds you in your own quiet
room,
glowing now like myself
hearts alive in their rhythm
of a song,
a chance to find where we belong,
in a brave world,
unquestionable beauty finds us
every step of the way,
the crater where the bombs hit my heart,
an empty abyss of passion

and no one could ever reach
the bottom,
desperate veins

in me swelling up forever,
lingering here for a few moments
hoping to find you,
war waged
and my only hope is to somehow
reach down
and find with intention but find unexpected passion
which will flow throughout this world
glow on with an energy unmatched
and unheard by the world although all of our ears are itching to hear

342

i hold a patient love in my hands
outlasting tempest,
bursting the waves
when the calmness of my dreams
seeks you
and memorizes all the places
where your skin was torn,
where the wounds
grow deep
love lies underneath
where the swell in my soul only
wants you, to fill all the empty spaces
lefts by these cuts,
the dream of my youth,
of purpose
find their home in your arms
where there are worlds to be built

a castle
a home
a guard, a place of rest
my life i would give for yours
i trade all the worlds
for a glimpse of your heart

343

the crowds
through these streets,
the paths that lead all of us,
across all worlds,
the simple
reaching of arms,
the letters
all across the world,
some of them i have sent myself,
reaching the eyes,
of those in need of a comforting word,
a trial,
a tribulation we've all walked this path,
my tortured soul

bereft off connection,
with those I long to hear,
my courageous
pen, my almighty heart,
my gracious enclosure,
my one last treasure,
my tools that I use,
to climb out of this place,
a life that I hold,
the world stays the same,
each moment trapped in time,
each star forever aligned,
greater love, championed between us,
guardians of our souls,
against
the iron and clenching grip of routine
of governments striving to seize us,
my heaven connected to yours,
all so far away,
dreams flow forever
into the future that calls to us,
the life of the world falls so far away,
we walk with our eyes closed

and repeat every day.

the music began to dim in
this city, and the clouds grew darker,
the birds all congregating in the sky,
watching our every deliberation,
the cycles of nature never releasing us,
stinging cold of the night sky,
greets us and beckons us into its nebula
and deep into its abyss,
the life of the world flows into
darkness, the path away from
here,
alive at long last,
in a place where hope finds a life

344

there is a chilled wind,
even now reaches
across all the oceans,
where dreams rest
and look up toward
the sky, looking for the birds
and a cure for the fear of mortality
a constant vexing force, the power of justice,
judged himself
we shall see then where we stand when the broken roads
were marked by our weary feet
carve a new path, long after
the visible road was destroyed.

345

weary hearts are welcome to rest here and make their abode
as long as they like
in my Inn, located in the center of all oceans
that these shipwrecked hearts travel hoping to find the

31

voice or even the solemn touch of another
touch is more than I can stand,
overwhelming in its current, bent toward
euphoria and peace,
this solemn sea that led us to this little
alcove here, where we can for a moment rest

346

the pages were once empty but now are overflowing
like a train
still eternally moving
but without mistake derailed
the lights that guided it are far away
and now, these pages
are filled with bitter images
of the wrath that floods my heart
life was derailed
With no warning at all,
hope crawls out of memory and is lost and never
finds its way home,
free my heart so that eventually I can find
my place at home and my voice in a song

347

there are shores
where ships arrive
the moonlight guided them here

all converging here,
conversing in their grace,

bitter winds have capsized souls who were not as lucky,

my grace falls into your folds of
unstoppable love,
the bitter struggle in this world
made my heart grow completely numb

the solace found here last,

the light against all darkness,
the all-consuming depth of passion,
consumed my body and soul,
burned to a crisp
from its engine and sway of reaching

the pertinacious power of my soul
together surrender, always holding
on to the demand,
of burning seething love,
forever

CD #12

the faithful heart
follows the firelight
into the void
where darkness shines,
where each night
drags on for a thousand years,
where the faithful heart,
always is drenched in tears,
hold my heaven close to you,
the journey through this ocean,
never seems to end,
the life of patience
flows with me,
in every gentle stride,
holding your heart to mine,
I find strength and power,
virtue clinging forward,
for what we have that is left,
come dream with me of the oceans

of the phantoms that have forsaken,
this once proud world,
that now lays at the mercy
and in ruins,
of those who hold the key,
to some cages but not their own,
of mortality, for what its worth,
pulls me on forever,
taking me where it wants to go,
drawing me to its goal,
the last power of my heart
was the ability to write,
to flow with words into song,
if only you could see me,
you would know
that my heart has come undone,

the praise of the natural world,
which we followed and drenched
our hands in its sands,
pull me closer to what you know
breathe for as long as you can sing,
greet me in the light of the darkness,
its welcoming and bitter glade,
where paths that lead us far from here
all alight with my sovereign

guidance,
follow me headlong into the future,
for what its worth,
away from violence
from the lights that I follow,
the joy in my hands,
hands touching hands,
hand always meant to hold,
all the things a person's hands
say about them,
thousand stories never told ,
of lives crawling through the cold,
of songs never sung,
of voices never perishing,
wars are never over,
just paths to more despair,
we can only look inward,
instead of from the outside looking in,
from the outside all looks different,
the whole world looks clear,
greet me in the moonlight
and tell me what you've seen,
all the souls you see here
are desperate to be free,
the final lamp in this dark,

i will find it in your heart,
those welcoming arms,

i've been seeking,
your open-compassionate heart
i know that somewhere
there's always room for me inside,
this will always be our Dominion,
a world separate from all others,
but the God of this world
we fled from, a master of many slaves,
to live is but to observe,
to thrive is not only to hear,
but to know and understand
emphatically to love,
the passion of the poets,
the liturgy of the birds and stars,
my sunlight calls to yours
somewhere across the world,
my moonlight drags me to sleep
and in sleep i never wake,
we are here celebrating
the life of the world
we defend what only belongs to us,

i always felt enamoured with
the light inside the darkness,
it doesn't admit it exists,
but is there for all to see,
every creature of this world is
good, not any part is vile,
my heaven comes to earth,
every time the blue bird lands,
and experiences the wind,
like i feel against my skin
this is poetry resounding,
the interconnection of abundant
wells of everything
we ever needed or wanted,
all of it guides us here,
my love in all this world,

to fall after what we crave,
to be so close to heaven
that we are all amazed,
of the precious gift of light,
that follows us through the dark,
where those who thought falsely
they could constrain us,
never accounted for
a certain mystical power

that leaves the rich empty handed
but never forsakes the poor,
greets them in the headlights
of a bright and burning star,
that leads us now and forever,
like the breath of passing cars,
leading me somewhere
but i cannot tell you
where i am going or who sent me,
all i can say with certainty
is that this is the path of peace,
the life of the world striving
to hold the light in hands,
it flitters so far when grasped,
never follows its possessor's demands,
a life of its own is swallowed,
in the heaven of the sway,
the breeze of all of the oceans,
mixing together today,
into something we can hold,
so tightly that our songs come undone,
i am here daydreaming,
with power in my hand,
writing across the world,
on the utter verge,

of holding heaven so close to me,
i will never forget

the days we spent together,
basking in the light of the sun,
the welcoming life of freedom
which we strive for every day
a Dominion, a land of our own
where we will greet
travellers passing by,
one day i too will be a passerby,
somewhere on the way,
the light guiding me forever,
my soul forever strained,
until i find what i seek,
until the stars fall from the sky,
and guide us with all the answers,
our empire was crafted by the divine
my life is but a shadow,
a vapor in the wind,
so come and greet the morning with me
each moment you touch me,
my soul comes alive again

349

always i dream of ships
crossing over to safer shores,
the deep glow of swelling
light of morning,
that wipes away all fears,
greets us in every space

grows closer
inevitably
in the harrowing
of all lights
with me to a
new world,
my desire,
to flee with these lights

all stars
growing close and i the scribe of these stars,
crafting out their tale
and their poem,
fly with me in the ocean of gracious welcome,
on a journey,
on a flight

these stars call to me
always,
the lights twinkling in their brilliance
the stunning passion of these stars
that led them on
to a world
unlike anything we've ever seen,

my passion grew while traversing
with these stars,
always,
seeking a home, a world where they can be together,

an understanding of where
these stars had fled off to,
was all I needed
to know at the end of our days,

the days of our lives
were always
guided by the stars

but these stars will be led by us
in the heart we hold

the lights grow dim
and we were close to the end
but our hearts were filled with joys and blood
beating in our hearts,
grew perfect and peaceful,

life we had fled to

350

the machine that claws
that digs into the sides of its victims

crushing weight of violence
pressing down on victims with no power
to fight back,
all consuming in its visceral hatred

its bitter destruction
flowing throughout all the world
centralized control

not only separating families
but dropping bombs on foreign homes

greet me in the morning
in the twilight of those same bombs

we will run off
to a world
unseen,
the light glistening against
the sea,
our journey is about to begin
we will be taken to a new world
which
has existed in a realm,
a little beyond our dreams,
dreaming was the first step
but never took us far enough,

we had only ever stood in the doorway

of the world where we belong
you were always the of my heart

the moonlight of the story
growing dim
but always
wanting to find a place where it can shine on peaceably
forever
the touch of the other enough
to remind us of the love that fell down
on us from the stars

351

the embrace
of sadness
takes me over
the future was ours
but can so easily be swept away
in the arms of quiet woods
i wait and hope its voice will take me far away where
i will never be found
better lost than found
the changes within the world are overwhelming

352

always remember
the memories that inspired
you in your youth

the decay of time
will slowly
batter at the memories
lessening their power

loosening their grip or hold in your mind

these memories
are the anchor
of your experience

within this world
the foundation
shaken
and no longer
any solid ground
to rely on
the heart goes on
when life is destroyed
i would know this most of all

but when the heart goes on
it never goes on the same

perishing hearts within this world
forcing themselves
each day

the genuine love of passing things
burns
up and expires
in the night but guides
our paths
that lead
to just outside its doors

353

waiting within
the airport
of forever
hoping to hear the call for
freedom,
the power that i crave

the calm oceans

that surround me echoing their
histories
their truth and my surrender to
these same mysteries

354

captivated
by the passage of time
and glow of tomorrow,
though faint,
guiding us
to foreign arrivals
where we can find a place
of rest and replenish
our minds
barraged by the winds of forever
calling to me,

the moonlight
crawls toward us slowly
graciously
and the heaven that calls to us

greets us forever,
all desire leads to one place
in one fulfilment,
one love,
one morning and one sacrifice
falling upon us

my life
was always torn between
what i've been seeking and the winds
pushing me the opposite direction,

the paths twist and turn guiding us away from where
we started,
the journey itself has
changed us
and restored our minds

44

the bright light of the morning calls
as the day comes
and our hearts are rejuvenated,
and once again whole

355

the machine marches on,
those who follow it lose
their eyes,
and eventually writhe in the
madness of perpetual darkness,
where there is no tangible path
out of the shade,
the light had flown so far away,
with the stars fleeing the sky,

somewhere, i don't know where,
in this same darkness,
there is dimly heard a melody
in the vast distance,
originating from the hearts
of the lost,

a heart beating even now courses through
all the world,
filling all spaces
with its patience
and its many certain promises,

grow with me in joy,
each day that world grows colder,
our hearts grow violent,
in their power and
mighty force that overthrows
the walls surrounding us,
the status quo of those
who will never change,
shaken to the core,
my love fills all the world,

45

unstoppably present,

the night falls upon the world,
and the true power in this
world belongs to us
together as the kings
and queens of this world
who know for certain
that the only power
ever comes from the heart,

the machine marches on,
and the nerves of this machine
can no longer feel
or understand,
the tempest of the wind battering
against hearts
but here i stand free as the
movements of the wind,

356

powerless to fight
against the regime of death
as we believe
as we wait in quiet rooms
for all time to end and for
the life in veins to expire

though in separate rooms
i will write letters
and send them to you

the birds will carry them
to where you sit
in shadows
somewhere
from the other side of the world

i took this power
in my clenched fists

and fought
tooth and nail
against the villains
who wanted to slay
those same birds that
guided my path

my arms can only
reach so far
but tonight
i imagine that they reach across
the worlds

my heart
healing begins
when memories
find me and take me to
the past

the life i had once known now gone
forever
burning rivers
of fire that severed worlds

when my heart is spoken

357

i hope for the dawn
which crawls towards me
all i can hope for is love
somewhere—i don't know where

358

i dream
of quiet mornings
where we fall in love,
with the life pulsing through the world
joy is our dream,
which we surrender

47

rather than face the firing squad
that the world has become,
destroy me
and my ashes will now and always triumph
over the world
lives spent
perpetually waiting for better days and warmer hearts,
vicious creatures
take the reins of our world
and pull,
crushing us with every crack of the lash

my heart, held close and unleashed,
upon those who happily made us victims,

my precious time
drifting through this world
and never seen or heard from again,
power reaching out
from my heart
and unleashed
as the breath of
my song,

the rhythm of creation,
its beat like a drum,
finding me in the place i reach for the sky
not to surrender but rather
to rise
to fight for a love
even if it costs me my life

359

the movement and flight of our lives

the tides of time
have taken us here we never
wanted to go,
my fleeting heart,
bursting forth

toward its certain tomorrows,
tomorrows always promise the unknown,
the light of our futures burn up and can never last,
the hell we've found ourselves in,
burns itself into extinction,
my lights shine out forever,
calling these
sojourners
who might seek the light
traveling through the woods
blindly in the darkness of the bright abyss,
hidden by the fog of darkness

if you can hear my champion song, listen
if but for a moment
and listen quietly
for the violence in the world
to be quenched
by those lost souls,
brandishing their newfound lights
in this world,
my tired eyes
struggle to see in this night,
blinded by the burning reflections
of the lost souls treading through
these woods
swaying in the
winds of this place
where so many souls
come together
rest with me
in this darkness as it calls in
the gracious memory of the distant past

my beautiful light
my only need
is to hear the sound
of the desperate heart,

the anxiety of a tortured heart fills
every empty spaces

in the world where joy is
not found

find me somewhere
waiting in these woods
until dawn comes
and the brightest of lights
shines through

360

O beautiful lights!

O beautiful love!

heaven's wind on my horizon,

bashing through
the clamoring future
of the anticipated
morning darkness
guide me somewhere
where i can hear eternity calling
darkness falling upon our worlds

our heaven's light
so far away

Jacob's ladder has no steps to climb

December's cold breaks in tonight,

my night of misery
follows me everywhere
threats of violence
in a desperate life
someone's beloved
threatened tonight

the power lies right above my heart
eternity approaches so slowly tonight

my mind is filled with words to overthrow

the demons
that pierce and rule the world

eternity calls no matter where my heart breaks

that is where it always calls me to stand

the everlasting flow of my bright morning calls me
to hold you close in the night

the valleys where we wait for tomorrow to come

tomorrow is forever taking its time
light of my path
a way through the mirage
of visions we will walk through them all and find a place of our own
a healing place,
a life away from the cold
bursting forth and ships all adrift,
fleeing to crevices in the ocean where we may never find them again.

361

the quietness of solitude
of the winds of peace
of the power and patience
to wait for the end of all time

the light of the dawn,
the silence that follows

the peace of our morning,
together we stood stronger,

the currents and winds of the chamber
where we would hide away together

holding love close,

memories pass forever

burned away
never again understood or conceived of
breakers of lamps
and now fire spreads
across the world
of mine
called by the name of the lamps that were broken
and their lights are silenced

what we added to our hearts led to our destruction,
of what we kept hidden,
away inside our souls

memories pass and never return,
when i fall down, i never arise,

all those who have arms should reach
for the skies
for what they can feel,
even if nothing at all,
the holes in our hearts were so small, but now
our hearts can hold nothing at all

362

the marks of my panic,
the emblems of my pain,
strewn across the world,
where you will find
in so few words,
the wrath that fills my heart,
the desperate life of darkness,
that follows us
in our trap,
where we panic and fear
we will never escape,
the world of darkness,
of burning buildings,
of a certain hope

that never appears,
that represents a future,
blown to bits,
a world afraid of its own shadow,
a hint of despair,
that flows through us like hell,
burning life in the woods craving
salvation, while I gaze toward the sea,
looking for a better life,
we may never find our future
life in veins tormented in a prison,
in a cell, watched
and invaded by prying eyes,
that see all heresies in the darkness,
itself the true heresy,
my life,
the perfect loaded gun,
that pervades all eternity,
breaks with its current forever,
of these waves,
that caress me violently,
unwavering panicked breaths,
wavering only to breathe,
taking in only as few breaths as necessary,
my immortal heart is open
for the world to see,
the sea so cold, frozen over,
which i can now gaze at and imagine,
the ships that have lost their way
in these same seas,
somewhere unable to find their homes,
broken souls, never resting,
their sunlight has long ago disappeared,
vanished in the light of the darkness
the loaded gun of my life
unloaded as rounds into the bottles in
the ocean,
containing the message of hope
for all of forever,
those lost soldiers out at sea,
whose words will never reach us,

my ultimate goal is to be made whole
by whoever can see or hear me,
the connection is simple
but is lost forever,
what is broken is not so easily fixed,
the heavy hand of those holding
their weapons falls down heavy upon us,
the weapons now blunted,
work all the same
heaven and hell are at war in this game,
the message that we tell you for all of our lives,

the flowing winds,
guiding these ships adrift to somewhere
they might belong,
unstoppable forces of governments,
their hammers, their sickles,
their bitter taste of their swords,
into the sides of the ones who hold the
true power,
nothing that can be done to take my power
from me,
my power exists through grace,

the moonlight of my life burns
and guides me in the shadows,
and the world does not know its own shadow,
but this shadow is immense,
covers all in darkness,
burns up when the arms of slavery
clasp our wrists
and claw into our ribs,
hold me like the memory of the ones who were lost not so
long ago,

Life has become an empty room,
and all those I have known have left,
have fled, like those from my country,
South Africa, an empty hell,
where in this nation,
my heart slowly empties,

i sit here and drink forever
from the bottle of wasted memories,
so i can always remember this shell
of a room that was once a nation,
of a nation that was once a home,
of a life that was born to be broken,
where lies grow in the bitter
horizon for this room,
of the power entrenched in my heart,
nothing i drank could erase this power,
no matter how hard i tried,
the room of South Africa was moving,
always pressing forward,
i could see all the places it was treading,
towards its judgment, towards its future,
the end of all days approaching,
the power in my heart burning,
its painful nature was clear,
my heart was about to burst,
the end of all worlds was near,
the nation would face its judgment,
and i alone would be left to account,
a judge and a priest and liturgy,
a nation of all birds and stars

363

walking away
and twisting off
every light,
and taking the batteries out,
storing these batteries
for when i need them,
only this will scare the demons away,
the bitter pill of life to swallow,
the vanguard of forever will be held up in arms with
weapons,
firmly possessed,
fueled by the batteries from the flashlights,
blunted trauma against
the darkness,

only violence will do,
violence with words,
our precious chart,
of the stars, guides us to
a home where we've always belonged,
longing for the truth,
of the source,
of all the true power and light,
find me
somewhere waiting here
to unstitch the patches of truth,
that were hidden somewhere
underneath your clothes,
hidden somewhere
in this room,
but life, its fullness,
i'm glad you're here,
with you i bet life wouldn't
be so bad,
hold me in the starlight,
hold me so close to your
candlelight,
guard me forever like there
is meaning
in the value of all precious things,
if you can hear me tonight
the saints
watch over us like birds,
the angels watching us like stars,
the power of
silence flows
through all sounds

364

O My Lord,
hold us here
in peace,
of the passionate
prayer of the one
far from his country—stranded

broken, battered bones,
nights swallowed in
eternity, in the cowering seas

a thousand voices
and their forgetting
of all the fullness of souls
forgetting of the light that used to guide us,
lead me to where
i can stand on my own feet,
where the fury if my heart blows over in all dreams,

when you left South Africa
there were a thousand voices

"don't come back. If Walmart was gone, you'd shrivel up and
die of starvation."

minds have left and never returned,
crisis of the soul,
deficit of love for the beautiful paradise,

surrounded by
the unwelcoming voices
these too seek dominion,
but the power flows forever
from my veins,
the love that flows through me,

i wish i could vanish with you,
disappear one day
and reappear in a new universe,

stories told of millions of cities
somewhere there across
those stars,
standing close to the border and gate, of where our future
begins,
the frightened life we live goes on,
and flows forever in its strain,
its current, connected to where it began, only God knows

if we will ever escape,
our future calls us
in our vision,
which we see in a moving room,
our faltering movements
as we try to leave this room,
but fall to the opposite side

through this window we can see,
scenes from our sylvan past
the world as it was, totally innocent,
we were children walking
through the woods at night,
but then there was violence,
torture thrust us down,
by figures in masks
treading our once peaceful woods
and threatening us with violence,
we fled and left for cities,
where we thought we might
finally be safe,
the wars began which we never started,
the life was descending
into the coldness of dark caverns
which we could not easily reach,

365

when all that is left is fear,
i do not know how i will make it
through the night
the terrors that fill the world,
outside our house
are paralyzing the mind,

greet me in the morning
and we will walk again
through all of those woods,
we will find a path to walk,
which we barely remembered from dreams,

we will find our lamp
in the dark,
our heaven's light of all
things, a token
fallen from above,
a future that called to us,

my burning heart
was never put out,
always searching for what brings
life to hearts
but silence floods the world,

stand with me in your gentle
night, passion blowing with the breeze,
windows open as we step outside,
together, and you take my hand,
be part of my nation, part of my story, a future to love and hold,

the birds guide us on a path
to where we will experience the world of the past,
learn about the history of this world,
the scabbard of my peace in the world, covers the weapon
of truth,
the way out is marked
by many tears, history of long-suffering in the night, a brilliant
spell of forever, its grace has
no beginning or end,
if i die they will not find me,
but you will find me when you take my hand,
walk with me somewhere you always wanted,
follow me to your cherished
seas, where we will watch the ships finally reach our shores
and you will return my heart
to me

forgotten letters
not all of them burned,
ashes of the letters
are dispersed and spread
so that no one will read them,
my fallen life descends deeper
into places of lament,
under the boot of governments
the passion of my night
embarking forever on a long
voyage through my future,
hold my heart close as
we travel, as we see distant lands disappear so far away,
i am the warrior who holds his
sword, and breathes freely
in the world of colors,
the light of the lampposts guide our
path, on all our journeys through these seas,
hold my heart close to yours
as we flow forward through the waves
the birds will guide us
as we float away, somewhere we
never stand united
never strive for freedom
south africa is not our land

we've always looked out toward the ocean imagining where it
might take us,
find me always longing and looking out toward the sea,
the future in the colors
of the dawn is covered by all the birds,
flying faster and farther than we can reach,
held stable by the arms that love us,
centered in our place by
the poems written on the walls of the library

i find myself in this room
where the cinematic scene
is outside our walls
playing on
the window
of past events and dreams
the room move like a rollercoaster
taking us for the ride,
as we see a thousand stories unfold
none of them are lies,
they greet us in their welcome
they take us far away,
come with me in the morning
take all my fears away
so that i can finally stand
and hold my self firm on this ground
my life will be but a memory,
my heaven covered in ifs shroud
if you will someday find me
in the visions of tomorrow,
my life was always spent running
always burning to escape
my heaven calls to you
the morning falls after us, if you can hold me closer,
if your closeness heals my heart,
know that time does not heal all wounds
we Lord knows it won't heal mine
if all time takes us far away
i will fall away from what i crave
the light of the world
stepping down into darkness
makes all the world burst in its day
follow me with your warm heart
where my nightmares will melt away
my future is dark without you,
it is covered in its night
fallen worlds collide
and become whole in their
places of truth,

life in spring
and futures to burn up,
in the heaven that calls us,
my power flows forever
in the simple places where words are unleashed,
the poems through the world
can be constrained by no force but truth,
may God save us from our misery
may our despair be hindered in its path
if all world are against me tonight
then all worlds will soon feel my wrath,
bend me until i am broken then
listen closely to me in this night,
hold me forever as one who always knew
how to walk the path
towards that city which we would from now on call our home,
away from the dark dominion,
away from unpleasant sceptre and throne

368

a creation
of life,
irreplaceable in this world
call me by your power
and meet me in the light

come as we watch the sunrise and look out
and watch the sea,
the boiling hearts forever
will evaporate in these seas,
fly with me as we run after the birds,
hold a candle to my night
be my guardian of the sea,
as worlds burn in the light,
nothing can contain the ocean, or
stop it from swallowing us where we stand,
the light of the world surrounds us,
prepares me and hearts of our voice,
to speak to the seas to whatever

force will hear me, as long as it has power to sing, thrive with me forever,
guide me
in your arms, as we stand on the bow of the ship,
the wind guiding us on our way
carve the path towards creation,
we will stand together even tonight
light of the world steps down into darkness
we are forever crawling toward the future tonight,
craving whatever we can grasp, holding whatever we find
there will be no paths forward
in a world led by the blind,
falling apart from the top down,
my power now is unashamed
hold me in the anthem of the sunrise
of the stars dissipating into the waves,

the creation from nothing
into what is perfect,
hold me forever tonight,
call me back to your melody,
where i can bask in the sound

the life of our story buried in sands, submerged
in its ocean one day,
call me to life from
the place i am lost
and never let me
return to that place,

my memories all fade to ashes with the wind,
like the fires where all the poems were burned
pictures of harmonie gone with the time, decayed in the winds of
our panic,
follow me closely my dear love,
hold me as an anchor tonight
the map of the seas, gone with the wind,
so we will only stand now as souls alone,
families come together and are united
by the force of their love,
nothing will ever keep us apart
the time has tortured all of us,

cities have burned in the night,
but if you hold me close
as the ship sails away
we will soon find our eternal home

For information on how you can help those in need in South Africa, regardless of race or religion, etc., please visit

feedsa.co.za

A journey of a thousand miles begins with a single step.
- Laozi, Chinese philosopher

Reminder that no one is unredeemable.

The Seven Chief Stars

Miguel
Mateo
Gabriela
Rafa
Rumas
Joruth
Jeremiah

The Five Chief Birds

Tatiana
Feliziano
Gabriel
Urius
Matthias

Joseph Leo Hickey III lives in Virginia.

He is the author of fifteen other poetry books. These
books include *Baptism of Apathy*, *Unity*, *Love Poems at the End
of Our Lives*, *Liefie*, *The Last Poem*, *Purity: Redeemed*, *The
Penultimate Poems*, *Harmonie*, *The Revenant*, *I Know Nothing but
Miracles: Walt Whitman Speaks to the Modern World*, *True
Daughter of This Soil*, *There's a Serenity in The Dark*,
Americanborn: Psalms of the Silent Nation, and *The Last &
Eternal Fire*, *American Poet: Elegy for the Light* and *Nuestra
Casa Eternal: Our Eternal Home*,

He is currently thirty-one years old.

YouTube: allthestarsaredead

joseph@melodiumhouse.com

Upcoming Poetry Books to be written or published by Joseph Leo Hickey III:

Anastasia's Crown, The Young Heart's Engraving, Baptism of Apathy: Portfolio 2 – As She Surrenders to Silent Seas, The Warmth of The Sun & Other Poems, No Greater Sorrow, No One Ever Truly Dies, The Red Ring of Fire Between the Stars, Poet of Body and Soul: Walt Whitman's Breath in the Modern World, GoneGirl: The Last Phantom, Voicemail Portfolio of Poetry: Untethered Voice, You Still Loved Us: Mysteries of Glorious Grace, Typewriter Portfolio of Poetry: Memories of Those Passing By, Unity: Portfolio Two (Working Title), Purity Portfolio 2: Dawn of a Dream, Emily Dickinson: Speaking the Future – Forever, Time Capsule: A Life Fulfilled, War: The Lasting Darkness, American Poet: The Life and Adventures of Jon Doe, American Poet: Galway Girl, American Poet: The Spell of Father Time (Working Title), American Poet: Satoshi, Baptism of Apathy: Portfolio Four, Baptism of Apathy: Portfolio Five, Baptism of Apathy: Portfolio Six, Baptism of Apathy: Portfolio Seven, Baptism of Apathy: Portfolio Eight, Baptism of Apathy: Portfolio Nine, Baptism of Apathy: Portfolio Ten, Baptism of Apathy: Portfolio Eleven, Baptism of Apathy: Portfolio Twelve, Baptism of Apathy: Portfolio Thirteen, Baptism of Apathy: Portfolio Fourteen, Rap Anthology, A Journey Through Time & Poetry, The Ballad of Jon & The Light, American Drifter: 1967, American Poet 2: Plight of the Revenant Nation, The Confessions

Banner of the Broken Cross Titles (Each part consisting of ten volumes of poetry books and one novel telling the same story)
1. *Storm of the Worlds*
2. *Dreadful King of Hell*
3. *The Eternal City*
4. *The Flight of the Beloved*
5. *The Secrets of the Bard-prophet*
6. *The Heart of the Teacher*
7. *The Resurrection of the Crown*
8. *The Song of the Sparrow*
9. *The Lamp & The Throne of Shadows*
10. *The War of the Consuming Fire*
11. *The Wrath of the Wayward Prince*
12. *The Path of the Teacher*
13. *The Triumph of Orthodoxy*

Harmonie, Liefie and Sanger will return in

The Empire of the Birds & Stars

+

The Liturgy of the Birds & Stars

www.ingramcontent.com/pod-product-compliance
Lightning Source LLC
Chambersburg PA
CBHW071931020426

42331CB00010B/2810